All You Wan
Kund

Ravindra Kumar, Ph.D.
(Swami Atmananda)

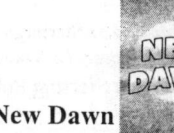

New Dawn

NEW DAWN
a division of Sterling Publishers (P) Ltd.
A-59, Okhla Industrial Area, New Delhi-110020
Ph.: 26387070, 26386209 Fax: 91-11-26383788
E-mail: ghai@nde.vsnl.net.in
Internet: http://www.sterlingpublishers.com

All You Wanted to Know About - Kundalini Yoga
© 2000, Sterling Publishers Private Limited
ISBN 81 207 2327 9

Reprint 2001, 2002, 2005

All rights are reserved. No part of this publication may be reproduced, stored in a retrieval system or transmitted, in any form or by any means, mechanical, photocopying, recording or otherwise, without prior written permission of the publisher.

Published by Sterling Publishers Pvt. Ltd., New Delhi-110020.
Lasertypeset by Vikas Compographics, New Delhi-110020.
Printed at Sterling Publishers (P) Ltd., New Delhi-110020.

Contents

Preface	4
Introduction	7
1. Understanding Kundalini	13
2. The Physiology of Kundalini	19
3. Methods of Awakening	28
4. Kundalini Yog	52
5. Symptoms of Awakening	58
6. Experiences of Awakening: Self-Realisation	66
7. Kundalini - A Common Basis of Most Faiths and Traditions	76
8. Chakras, Nadis and Kundalini Yoga in other Faiths and Traditions	91
9. Preparatory Microcosmic Orbit	115
10. First Exercise	123
11. Second Exercise	145

Preface

Kundalini yoga is a specialized form of yoga which in general combines *hatha, tantra, mantra, laya* and *raja yogas* scientifically, in a way. It is aimed at stimulating the "dormant energy" at the base of the spine, called *Kundalini* in the East, and *Spiritual Life Force* in general. Kundalini, on awakening, passes through the seven centres of energy called *chakras*. The lowest, below the base of spine, called *Mooladhar*, and the highest, on top of the head, is called *Sahasrar*. When it reaches the highest centre, one perceives higher consciousness, experiences it and lives in it, finally.

This book defines kundalini, discusses various methods of awakening and ways of recognizing it, and the precautions and self-realisation, as a result of the awakening. I express my gratitude to the authors whose works I have consulted. However, the text is based on my personal experiences which led to the formation of the 'Academy of Kundalini Yoga and Quantum Soul'. I wish to thank Jytte

Kumar Larsen for the use of computing facilities and related help.

Swami Atmananda (Ravindra Kumar, Ph.D.)
Founder President
Academy of Kundalini Yoga and Quantum Soul
58-61 Vashisht Park, Pankha Road,
New Delhi-110046
Tel: 5047091, 5041368, 5034143, 5137567

Introduction

Some people write inspiring prose or poetry and some compose beautiful music while others cannot; some students perform brilliantly in examinations with little effort while others, in spite of long hours of work, score poorly; some people are famous for wonderful discoveries and inventions while others live mediocre lives and die unnoticed. What is the "factor" which is responsible for these outstanding differences? The answer is *kundalini*.

Almost all faiths and traditions of the world have had some knowledge of this energy, although the names for definition and the extent of exploration have been different. Researchers have been looking for a common ground and Perennial Philosophy has been found to be the highest common factor, representing the metaphysical system of the prophets, saints and sages.

According to Aldous Huxley, it is perfectly possible for people to remain good Christians, Hindus, Buddhists, or Moslems and yet be united in full agreement on the basis of doctrines of the perennial philosophy. A systematic representation of this philosophy is found in the *Bhagavad Gita*.

As we would later see, kundalini is at the root of an enlightened person, whatever his faith or tradition. Although a mathematician, I had an equal interest in the field of spiritual research. Interacting with people of various religions in about ten countries, where I taught mathematics, has provided me an opportunity to gather data supporting the theory that there is a common thread running through all of them, which eventually leads one to search for inner peace and God.

In 1994, I resigned as a mathematics professor from the University of Tanzania, as my interests shifted to religion and parapsychology. I experienced the awakening of the kundalini in 1987 and have been writing the "truth" in a series of papers published in the U.S.A.

The timeless *Vedas* have prescribed three specific paths for searching the "truth": *bhakti-yoga* or the path of devotion for those who have their heart more developed than the mind; *jnana-yoga* or the path of knowledge for those who have their mind more developed than the heart; and *karma-yoga* for those who have a balance between the heart and the mind. In medieval ages, Guru Gorakhnath and others discovered *hatha-yoga* for those who have neither the heart nor the mind developed to lead to the awakening of the kundalini.

Kundalini-yoga is in fact a combination of all approaches, it has a systematic and calibred scale of evolution, and it is claimed to be the shortest path to God.

This book deals with this subject in appropriate details suitable to those who have little time to read seriously and yet want to know the subject reasonably well. The text is based on my own experiences and Sterling Publishers deserve thanks for their bold step to present the truth in this short form.

Understanding Kundalini

It was discovered that every individual has a special form of energy, which was found to be dormant in most, slowly evolving in some, and fully awakened in few. This energy has no form or dimensions but it has infinite capabilities.

It has been given many different names in various traditions, perhaps the Hindus have the oldest record of naming this energy *kundalini*. The name *kundalini* comes from the word *Kunda* which means cavity, representing the concave pit in which the human brain nestles in the form of a coiled serpent. In males, it lies asleep in the perineum, between the excretory and urinary organs. In females, it lies at the root of the uterus, in the cervix. It is imagined as a sleeping serpent coiled three and a half times, closing the opening of the *sushumna* nerve by its mouth in the centre of the spine.

Energy is of two kinds: potential and kinetic. In the potential form kundalini represents *shakti* or dormant power, while in the kinetic form it manifests itself as a female deity. When it is newly awakened and not yet under control, it is represented by the ferocious female deity Kali, who is naked, dark, and wears a rosary of 108 human skulls, the latter representing past lives. The blood-red lolling tongue of Kali represents *rajo guna*, signifying creative activity, and it exhorts the practitioner to have a control on his/her *rajo guna*.

When properly awakened and under control the kundalini is represented by the female deity Durga, who emerges as the higher, more refined and benevolent form of the unconscious. The practitioner can now make use of it for useful purposes and become powerful on its account. Goddess Durga is beautiful, charming and seated on a tiger. She has eight hands representing the eight fold elements of a human being. She wears a rosary of human heads, representing her wisdom and power. The 52 heads in the rosary represent the 52 letters of the Sanskrit alphabets and also represent the external manifestation of the "unstruck holy sound" called *naad* by the Hindus, *word* by the Christians, *kalma-i-ilahi* by Moslems, *music of spheres* by the great,

Pythagoras and so on. Durga is the superconscious form of kundalini, it signifies the burning away of karma, accumulated from several life times. The root centre-mooladhar is awakened, removing evil consequences of life and bestowing peace and power.

Efficient consciousness is represented by a serpent in many faiths and traditions. As for its three coils; it represents the three parts of *AUM (OM)* - past, present and future; three *gunas* (virtues) - *tamas* (under inertia), *rajas* (creative activity), and *sattva* (purified form); three states of consciousness -

waking, sleeping and dreaming; and three types of experiences which are subjective, sensual and absence of an experience. The half coil corresponds to the "dot" in OM, and it represents the state of transcendent consciousness which is beyond waking, sleeping and dreaming. Thus, the complete set of experiences of the universe followed by the experience of transcendent consciousness, are represented by three-and-a half coils of kundalini or three-and-a half branches of OM.

The Physiology of Kundalini

After the physical, astral, and mental bodies or planes one comes to causal body or plane, to which kundalini belongs. Thus kundalini exists in an abstract form only and it is beyond the concept of object, time and space. Its presence can be felt through its manifestations in the form of peace, tranquility, cosmic consciousness, detachment from worldly objects and relations, paranormal powers in some cases, and so on. It is comparable in some sense to electrical energy whose presence can be felt only through its manifestations, such as switching on a bulb, or a fan and so on. There are seven centres of energy called *chakras*, through which Kundalini passes. Transformation and transcendence of personality takes place with the opening of each chakra. This is a complete subject by itself and requires a separate dealing. However, a brief account of the chakras can be given as follows.

A *chakra* is a sort of junction where the nerves meet, like an

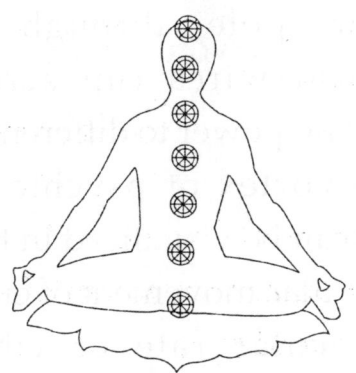

The Chakras

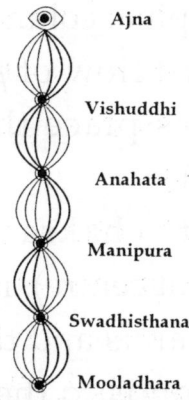

Formation of chakras through crossing of Ida, Pingla and Sushumna nerves.

electric pole through which electrical wires run across for supplying power to different places. It is a vortex of psychic energy which can be visualized in the form of a circular movement of energy, at a particular rate of vibration. Chakras are situated in the inner walls of the spinal column. Forward and backward flow of *prana* (vital energy) takes place through the *nadis* (nerves).

The first chakra is called *mooladhar* (root centre), it is situated between the anus and the genitals, and corresponds to the coccygeal plexus of the nerves. It controls the excretory and sexual functions in the body. There are lower chakras below the root centre going down to the heels. It is at mooladhar that the consciousness rises above the animal nature.

The second chakra is called *swadhishthan* which is situated just below the spinal column, and it corresponds to the sacral plexus of nerves. It controls the consciousness in a person.

The third chakra is called *manipur*, it is situated at the navel level in the spine, and it is related to the solar plexus of nerves. It takes care of the digestive, assimilative and temperature controlling system of the body.

The fourth chakra is called *anahat* (heart centre), it is situated at the back of the heart near the base in the vertebral column, and is related to the cardiac plexus of the nerves. Heart, lungs, the diaphragm, etc., are taken care of by this chakra.

The fifth chakra is called *vishuddhi* (throat centre), it is situated at the level of the throat pit in the vertebral column, and it is related to the cervical plexus of

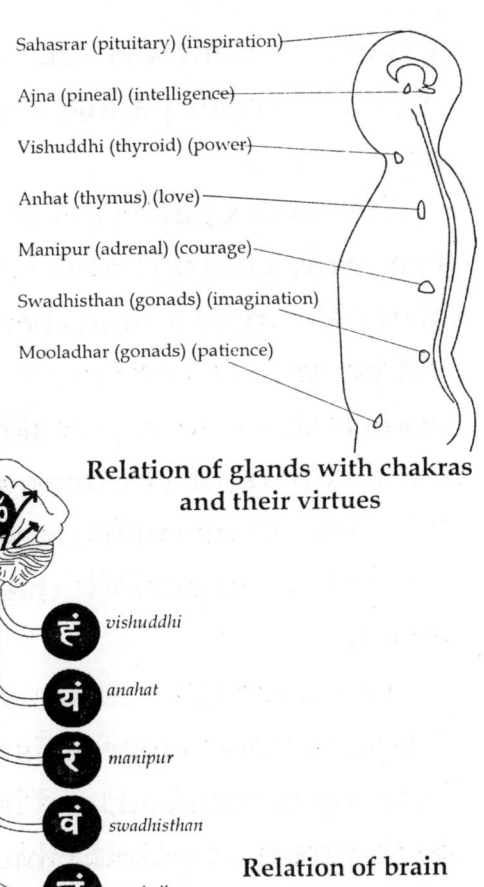

Relation of glands with chakras and their virtues

Relation of brain centres with chakras

nerves. It controls the thyroid complex, upper palate, epiglottis, etc.

The sixth chakra is called *ajna* (eye-brow centre), it is situated in the middle of the brain behind the mid point between the eye brows, and is related to the pineal gland. It is the centre of command and it takes care of most of the functions of one's life, especially the sexual activity.

The seventh chakra is called *sahasrar* (crown centre), it is situated at the top of the head, and is related to the pituitary gland which itself takes care of all other glands and systems of the body. It is the terminal point of the journey of kundalini and is the seat of cosmic awareness.

There is supposed to be an additional chakra between the sixth and the seventh called *bindu* (point), it is situated at that point on the head where the Hindus keep a tuft of hair, and it takes care of the optic system. On awakening this chakra, *amrit* (nectar) emanates, which rejuvenates the whole body of the yogi.

Methods of Awakening

By Birth

Rare persons are born with an awakened kundalini. There are mainly two categories in this type — first, a person born with a partial awakening is called a *saint*, and this could mainly be the reason that his/her process was left incomplete in the previous lifetime; two, a person born with full awakening is called an *avatar* or incarnation.

Such persons are calm, detached, loving to all, carefree, etc. They have clarity of vision and philosophy of high order. They are born metaphysical teachers.

Vedic Methods

There are three basic methods taught by the *Vedas*:

Bhakti Yog
- The path of devotion, is for persons in whom heart is more developed than the mind.
- Such persons visualize, think and feel that the Lord is present before them and they pour out their heart's love to God in various ways.

- Eventually, a continuous flow of awareness moves between the practitioner and his/her cherished form of God.
- Kundalini awakens and there is an awareness of relationship between the devotee and the Lord — twoness. Higher consciousness and a deep state of samadhi is experienced.

Jnana Yog
- The path of wisdom, is for persons in whom the mind is more developed than the heart.
- Such persons withdraw their mind and emotions from

perceiving life and oneself in a deluded way, so that one may behold and live in attunement with the "Spirit". One questions, "who am I?".

- Whenever a thought or feeling arises, which is not the goal, the practitioner says, "neti, neti" — "not this, not this", and discards the sense distraction, concept, image or sound, until the mind is clear and soul is revealed.

Karma Yog

- The path of selfless action, is for persons whose heart and mind are supposed to be equally

developed. Perform the action but not be concerned with the fruit, is the doctrine which is followed.
- They believe that there is a cause for every thing, and their situation in life is the result of causes they entertained and enacted.
- They establish new causes for a finer and more fulfilling life by changing their thoughts and feelings which supplant old habits and attitudes.

Hatha Yog

- There are also a large number of people who have neither the heart nor mind well developed. Consequently, Guru Gorakh Nath and others developed Hatha Yoga in medieval ages.
- Through yogic exercises one can develop a healthy body and pursue the goal of spiritual realization.
- Through clear mind and healthy body one can meditate and harmonize the body currents of feeling, thinking, willing and acting.

- A long list of *asanas* (yogic postures) has been developed by the yogis which can awaken the Kundalini through a regular practise.

Mantra Yog
- A smooth, risk-free, and powerful method is through the repetition of a mantra, which could be syllables, words or phrases, such as *OM Namah Shivaya*.
- It requires time, patience and guidance of a guru. Just as a stone thrown into a lake creates circular ripples, even so a *mantra*

repeated a million time creates vibrations in the ocean of mind.
- Eventually it develops the vision of a "higher force" and enables one to live in the midst of sensualities of life with an indifference towards them.
- There are a large number of mantras from Sanskrit which can attune one to the Lord and connect one to the realms of "higher consciousness".
- Each mantra is usually a result of revelations by some deeply meditating adept. Kundalini awakens methodically and systematically.

Raja Yog

- It is the "kingly path" which usually follows the practice of Hatha Yog and "vedic methods" for a reasonable time so that the mind has been stabilized, karmas are de-activated and emotions have been purified.
- Great sage, Patanjali has laid down eight limbs: *yama, niyama, asana, pranayama, pratyahar, dharana, dhyana* and *samadhi*.
- A sequential process of concentration, meditation and communion leads to the experience of union with the Absolute.

- As the consciousness develops in the "third eye", one begins to see pastel colours in the mind's eye: green, pink, blue, indigo, purple, yellow and white— nearly in this order. One day the light in the forehead "blazes brighter than the sun". One has to be careful not to overstrain the mind with excessive concentration, which can create a split.
- A true Raja yogi lives by the truth of the Bible: *If therefore thine eye be single, thy whole body shall be filled by light;* and lives in "bliss", having surrendered his will to God.

Path of Austerities (Tapasya)

- *Samskara* and *vasana* are eliminated by observing austerities.
- Dirt, complexes, and any behaviour causing pain and suffering are eliminated gradually.
- However, old habits are hard to go. Abandoned in a waking state, they begin to appear in dreams and later in the behaviour or in the manifestation of diseases.
- Matter is finished when will-power makes a decision, and this is the fruit of austerities.

- Karmas of many incarnations precipitate to the surface. For example, sexual fantasies may haunt the mind for long, one may become lean and thin or sick.
- Extra-sensory perceptions and paranormal powers (siddhis) may develop at this stage.
- The path of austerities is a powerful method and it cannot be handled by everyone.

Deep Breathing (Pranayam)
- Breath control with the three locks — root lock, navel lock and chin lock — practised regularly under ideal physical conditions

awakens the kundalini rapidly through the creation of yogic fire.
- One should be prepared physically, mentally, emotionally and philosophically to handle the power of the awakened kundalini, otherwise it can misfire.
- It is a direct method and can be explosive.
- Some centres in the brain can be awakened which can hinder the production of sperm and testosterone.
- As such, purification of the body through the prescribed methods

is recommended before one can take to the direct method.

Use of Herbs (Aushadhi)

- It is a quick method which can result in full or partial awakening of kundalini. But certain herbs can awaken the Ida or Pingla nerves, while others can suppress these nerves leading one to a mental asylum. As such, a guru is necessary for guidance.
- Marijuana and LSD are not the herbs which can excite the kundalini. *Somaras,* which is mentioned in the Vedas, is a juice extracted from a creeper in a dark

lunar fortnight on a particular day. It is then put in an earthen pitcher and buried in the ground until the full moon. This juice is responsible for inducing higher consciousness, visions and spiritual experience. Kundalini awakens and one goes into a state of samadhi.

- Some people like this method because sex drive is fully eliminated through the use of herbs.
- A disciplined life prior to the use of herbs is very necessary so as to avoid damage to the brain.

Laya Yog

- The practitioner locates the seven chakras in the body, preferably with the help of a teacher, and then these centres are used as "doorways to different realms of higher consciousness."
- People who have not opened these centres live on the three lower levels of consciousness - material, sensual and egoistic.
- Each centre on opening brings a specific transformation in the physiology.
- Over stimulation of a centre can cause pain and confusion on one

hand, and create intense desires on the other.

Kriya Yog

- A safer and practical method which does not confront the mind is kriya yog.
- It is more suitable for the householders since raja yog is meant for purified (sattvic) and disciplined people. Kundalini does not rise violently.
- It wakes up peacefully and rises slowly upwards.
- It is a process of awakening and reversion, so one sways between opposite experiences, such as,

eating too much at one time and very little at another time.
- Sometimes one experiences insomnia while at other times one sleeps a lot. It involves a set of yogic asanas (postures) and leads to spiritual experiences in a controlled way.

Tantra Yog

- It is the quickest way to awaken the kundalini, provided the practitioner has rightly understood the two principles of nature — Shiva and Shakti, and has transcended passions so that urges are not lurking within him/her.

- The goal of tantra is to harmonize the male and female aspects within, balance the masculine intelligence and feminine sentiments in oneself; and the moment this balance is reached, spiritual realization takes place. The whole universe is taken to be the expansion of the cosmic mother or the divine life force — spirit.
- Having purified one's heart and mind of worldly thoughts and desires, the practitioner senses the life force within and directs it to rise up the spine, from tail bone, to neck, to forehead.

- One overcomes long-formed harmful habits, such as, smoking, drinking, and overeating by replacing the pleasure derived from them with God's joy. Only misguided people relate tantra to sex and abuse it.
- A true tantric has already transcended sex completely. Sexual energy has been converted into spiritual energy.
- Awakening and transformation takes place slowly and unknowingly.

Shaktipat
- Samadhi is experienced through an instant awakening when an adept or guru passes his/her vibrations into the practitioner by touch, by looking, through a rosary, a flower, a fruit, a handkerchief, a dream, a letter, or a phonecall, etc., depending on the system mastered by the adept.
- One performs yogic postures without learning, begins to know mantras and scriptures from within, and physical transformations begin to take place in him instantly.

- This is called shaktipat, giving a glimpse of the reality, but it is not a permanent event. Eligibility for shaktipat does not depend on one's social or immediate conduct, but on the point of "spiritual evolution" one has reached, beyond which shaktipat can be effective.
- The way of one's eating, behaving, living, etc., depends on one's education and the way one has been brought up.
- One may be living as a renunciate for long and yet not be qualified, whereas an ordinary looking person may have

reached the point of transformation internally.

Conclusion

The methods can be divided into two broader categories: mild and safe, such as Bhakti yoga and karma yoga; and tantric methods which are fast though a bit risky.

In slower methods, the mind has to work as a schizophrenic, one wants to do or have some thing, but one negates it or suppresses it with the same thought or mind.

In fast tantric methods, one lives an open life and maximises effects by all possible ways.

Tantric methods are like a helicopter or LSD, fast though risky, with the possibility of a quick awakening. One can choose what one wants. Mostly the choice is automatic, according to one's grooming from the beginning.

Results of kundalini awakening have been observed by scientists. They have found maximum electrical charges in the spinal column for a person who has practised breath-control or pranayama.

Kundalini Yog

Although each specific form of yoga — bhakti, jnana, karma, hatha, mantra, raja, tapasya, pranayama, aushadhi (herbs), laya, kriya, tantra and shaktipat - has the capability of awakening the kundalini; a single method is time consuming and it has its own difficulties and limitations. Kundalini yoga combines most of them in a balanced and scientific way so that the awakening takes place swiftly and without problems, and in a single lifetime. There is a balanced development of personality: physical, mental, emotional and spiritual. A variety of diseases, especially the ones enumerated under "stress management" are systematically eradicated as a natural by-product of the awakening. Practice the following combinations given:

Hatha
Siddhasana, dhanurasana, bhunjagasana, ardhamatsyendrasana, vajrasana, sheersh-asana, etc., are to be mastered.

Pranayama

Deep-breathing with three locks: root lock (moolbandha), navel lock (uddayanabandha), chin lock (jalandharbandha), to be combined with siddhasana gradually.

Shashankasana

Special tool to balance breathing through two nostrils, inducing tranquillity of mind which is like a preparation for meditation/samadhi.

Laya

Having awareness of the seven chakras in the body, chanting OM and concentrating on the position of third-eye between the eye brows.

Mantra

Chanting of the mantra *OM Namaha Shivaya* with a technique of raising the voice and attention from the root centre to ajna centre.

Kriya

Concentrating attention from root centre to ajna and sahasrar, imagining the rise of kundalini, inviting God as liquid white light through crown centre and passing it into every part of the body with full awareness.

Tantra
Guiding married couples to live in a way which can catalyze the whole process.

Jnana
Reading scriptures and case histories of successful people on the path of yoga, and questioning the self — "Who am I?"

Shaktipat
Learning the technique of receiving God's vibrations directly from Him.

Samadhi
Practising pratyahar, dharna, dhyan which would lead to samadhi with an experience of bliss.

The whole programme is divided to be followed on different days of the week, and also on different times of a day, according to the suitability of the practitioners.

Symptoms of Awakening

Some of the common symptoms through which one can say that the kundalini has awakened in a person are given below. However, not all the symptoms will appear in every one rather, different symptoms will appear in different people according to their interests and training.
- Just as a self-starter in a car shakes the whole car with a small sound of thunder before the engine begins to operate, even so, when the first chakra at root or

the mooladhara awakens, the whole body shudders, one takes deep breath, and the body goes into certain yoga posture(s) spontaneously. One should give up the practices at this stage and should simply witness the changes happening.
- The life-force (prana) begins to rise upwards through the spine and repetition of mantra arouses blissful feelings in oneself.
- In some cases, trembling of the body, hair standing on end, involuntary laughing or weeping, seeing frightening

visions, uttering deformed sounds, or even ejaculations of semen have been observed.

- Automatic posture and fixing of gaze on the third eye, calming down or cessation of breathing and tranquillity of mind can be seen as the result of kundalini awakening.
- Performing an asana with root, navel, and chin locks involuntarily and/or the Khechri-mudra, the body becomes over active with energy.
- One also hears the unstruck sounds internally and goes into the state of samadhi.

- One indulges in involuntary physical actions of the body such as, rotation of the body like a grinding stone, jumping like a frog, or lying on the ground like a dead person.
- Some people lose control over their limbs as they jerk it forcibly, when they sit and close their eyes. Some people also utter unfamiliar sounds or the sounds resembling those of some animals.
- Some people feel that a spirit has taken possession of their body as they can involuntary perform certain yoga postures without

pain or fatigue, and also possess buoyant energy.
- Vibrations of life energy (prana) at different centres in the body, makes one feel that the energy is flowing in the direction of one's thoughts, and one feels electrical jerks in the nerves.
- A feeling of ecstasy and joy pervades one when one sits for prayers, sings hymns, or recites poetry in languages hitherto unknown. Sometimes they shake hands and/or clap rhythmically.
- One feels that the life force (prana) is active in the body, day and night, and a feeling of joy

and bliss permeates throughout, even in sleep.
- Fast movement of the body can be sensed while one is walking. One feels buoyant and joyful, attains an undisturbed balance of mind and one finds inexhaustible energy for work within oneself.
- The arousal of kundalini makes one feel intoxicated with the love of Divine, steps fall majestically while walking, and one feels a desire for solitude.
- One is able to see divine visions, inhale divine smells and tastes, hear divine sounds, experience

divine touch, and also receive instructions from "inner guru", while in meditation.
- The gaze fixes on the third eye while one performs khechari mudra. Cessation of breathing and diving into the ocean of bliss, is experienced as a result of "savikalpa samadhi".
- The scriptures are revealed while, the secrets of future are unravelled. All doubts are put to rest as one acquires strange powers of oration and self-confidence, so much so, that one does not feel the need of even contacting God.

- Body, mind, and prana get charged with divine influences at regular times all through the day.

Experiences of Awakening: Self-Realisation

The *yogis* discover great possibilities of life after freeing the body from tension and from the ravages of stress, and getting rid of mental and emotional turbulence gradually. The result of yoga is a miraculous well-being for the self, and a new unity between the self and others is like a "new beginning" for the first time. However, it is advisable to find a teacher since no book can replace personal coaching by an experienced one. One has to choose the kind of yoga which is suitable to oneself, since every one has a different grooming and way of life. No two people in the world have the same finger prints. In any case, Kundalini yoga is a combination of different important kinds of yoga and is suitable to every one for this reason. It develops the individual equally in all the four directions: physical, mental, emotional and spiritual. And there is a scale of measurement which can tell one about the progress that one has made so far and what is expected to happen next.

Whatever spiritual path one may follow, one experiences a "great explosion" due to the awakening of the kundalini, sooner or later, which transports one into another plane of being. It is a journey from the known to the unknown; ordinary consciousness becoming transcendental through the transformation of perceptions, feelings and experiences change as the kundalini passes through different chakras.

As the kundalini rises, appetite for food, and sleep slowly decreases, the mind becomes tranquil, one begins to see lights of different colours between the eyebrows and also hears various sounds. The five negatives — lust, anger, greed, attachment, and ego get precipitated in degrees but soon subside. Some practitioners obtain psychic powers like clairvoyance, clairaudience, telepathy, telekinesis, the ability to heal, precognition, levitation, etc., but these powers are short-lived and one should not pay any attention to them. Visions, poetic emotions, artistic perceptions, etc., can also be observed in variations and one often makes use of them in self-expression. Some people experience terrible headaches, but this generally happens to those who did not have sexual interactions of any kind in life. All these manifestations can be seen because the brain, which was hitherto active to only about 10 to 20 per cent, now experiences the awakening of its silent areas. Headache may thus be compared to the labour pain of a woman, since the yogi is now giving birth to spiritual consciousness.

However, the storm settles down gradually and one begins to live a normal life, externally, like others but internally, the awareness becomes very vast, transcending the normal categories and the scope of knowledge becomes greater. One may develop a special kind of genius, such as, philosophy and oratory, which may have a magnetic influence on people. A yogi also suffers from insomnia but it is welcome as one can use the extra time available for constructive purposes.

Evolution of consciousness takes millions of years; similar to our growing from baby, to child, to young man, to middle-aged-man, to old man; but if suddenly a child finds that he/she has become an old man with corresponding symptoms, such as, grey hair and wisdom; how will he/she feel? How will he/she cope with the situation? This is what happens to a person on the awakening of one's kundalini. However, with the growth of accompanying detachment (vairagya) this transition becomes smooth and the storm settles down gradually.

According to a verse in *Rigveda*, God and human soul are born simultaneously from the womb of a mother, like two twins. Another verse compares the two with two birds sitting on the same tree i.e. the physical body. One of them eats the fruit and falls into bondage, while the other watches without attachment. God, being eternally free and unaffected always remains by the side of the soul as his twin-brother. Separateness of the entities is false and one believes in this notion due to ignorance from self-created limitations of Maya. At a certain time when the soul sees God, it becomes free from worldly bondage. This is what happens after the awakening of the kundalini. Karmas accumulated from several life times are burnt, one is freed from the chain of incarnations of earth, and one proceeds to live on a higher realm after completing the formalities of this life time.

Such a person is called self-realized. He/She is always cheerful because his/her happiness does not depend on external factors anymore. The source of happiness or bliss which was within has now opened up. One acquires perfect health as a natural by-product and looks much younger than one's real age. One is not afraid of death, since one has died already in the process of meditation, and one has seen one's afterlife too. These things may not be understood at an ordinary level, but they can be found in most religions as a common denominator, and I can vouch for them through my personal experiences.

Kundalini: A Common Basis of Most Faiths and Traditions

Parapsychologist and religionist, Rober Winterhalter published his work *New Thought and Vedanta* in 1993. He pointed out the remarkable similarity between ancient Hinduism and the teachings of Jesus of Nazareth. Swami Ramakrishna Paramahansa said that all religions are the different means to the same end.

Repetition of the name of God is called "chanting of *mantras*" in Hinduism and Buddhism. Similar practices exist in other religions too. Chanting serves two purposes: it tires the mind from wandering aimlessly thereby, helping us to concentrate, and the hidden power of mantra evokes the forces of nature around and finally arouses kundalini. Arousal of kundalini opens "third eye" and a contact with the higher realms is established. Understanding God then starts as an ongoing process. There are marked symptoms of kundalini arousal from which the process is recognized.

St. Teresa of Avila sometimes experienced extreme heat, energy, spontaneous body movements and pain, which are the symptoms of kundalini awakening. Julian of Norwich fell gravely ill and experienced a death like feeling. She reportedly felt the lower part of her body die away and had such extreme pain that if she had known before, she would not have asked for it. However, she saw God in the twinkling of an eye and later meditated for twenty years. Similar happenings have been reported by King Bushman of Africa, Sufi saint, Taoist and Shamans. On the road to Damascus, St. Paul was blinded by a brilliant light from heaven for about three days, and he lived without food and water. On recovering his sight, he was converted to Christianity. The founder of Islam, Mohammed, was awakened one night by an overwhelming light which opened his paranormal eye and the revelation of the *Quran* began.

Such experiences with light in the kundalini process have been described vividly by saints, such as, Swami Muktananda and Swami Yogananda. They have also described visits to higher planes in bodily form which is similar to that of Mohammed. It is with a reference to these realms that Jesus said, "There are many mansions in my father's house." Swami Prabhupad, the founder of the International Society for Krishna Consciousness in United States, gives similar details in his book, *An Easy Journey to Other Planets*. Taoism and Vajrayan Buddhism have given elaborate techniques for manipulating the enormous heat generated by the awakening of kundalini.

In Sufism, a 'short path' to God is taken through *faqr* (pious poverty), studying religious literature and prayer with *dhikr*, that is, endless repetition of holy names of God and sacred passages from *quran*, leading to self-hypnosis, like the chanting of mantras. Sufis use prayer beads which are similar to the rosaries of Hindus. Rhythmic drum beating and dancing sometimes accompany *dhikr* to bring on a state of trance.

According to Idries Shah, freemasonry began with the

teachings of Spanish Sufi Iba Masarra and the three tools in the masonic emblem symbolize the three Sufi postures of prayer. He further said that Boaz and Solomon, builders of King Solomon's temple in Jerusalem, were Sufi architects. An unfinished tower and an eye on a dollar bill of America represent incomplete humanity being watched by the overall eye of God. Clearly, freemasonry had a great influence on American thoughts.

In Judaism, Kaballah, the short path to God, is supposed to have been taught by God to angels, then to Noah, Abraham and Moses, who finally initiated seventy elders. The *Merkabah* mystics endeavoured to reach the "God's Chariot" after passing through *seven heavenly mansions;* parallel to the seven chakras in kundalini process. The process includes fasting with repeated recitations of hymns and prayers to induce a state of trance. It is similar to meditation with the chanting of mantras leading to samadhi. Practical Kabulism introduced by Aaron Ben Samuel in Italy further spread to Germany and became the basis of *Hasidism*. It involved prayers, contemplation and meditation leading to witnessing the Divine Fire, *Shekinah* (likened to Shakti of Hindus), the mother or female aspect of God. Classical Kabullah was born in France and moved to Spain in the thirteenth century. The *Sefer ha-Zohar*, meaning the Book of Splendour, was written by Spanish Kabbalist, Moses de Leon. Another 'short path', named *Tzeruf*, was developed by Abraham Ben Samuel Abulafia in Spain. It was performed at midnight and involved breathing techniques, recitation of sacred names of God and meditation. The ecstasy, called *shefa*, meaning divine influx, would occur in short time.

Experiences are similar to the awakening of kundalini, including the unlocking of the "holy sound" leading to enlightenment and, perhaps illumination. Luria stressed the need of letter combinations (*mantra*) as an effective way to mystical prayers and meditation. Dion Fortune called Kabbalah the "Yoga of the West". The Christian Kabbalah was introduced by Cornelius Agrippa Von Netteshheim in his *De Occult a Philosophia* written in 1531.

The 'short path' in Hinduism, Buddhism and Zen practices is called 'Tantra' which includes yoga, meditation, and recognition of sex drive. Not only in the East but in the West too, a large number of practitioners have achieved higher consciousness, such as Alexandra David-Neel, Alan Watts, Alister Crowley and others, through tantra.

Experience of kundalini type are also found in the esoteric teachings of Egyptians, Chinese and some native Americans. In the *Bible*, it is interpreted as "the solar principle in man." Similar references can be found in the *Quran,* and in the work of Greek philosophers, especially Plato, Rosicrucian and Masonic writings. In Alchemy, *ching* (sexual energy) was converted into *chi* (sublimation of sex) through controlled breathing, and *chi* was made to circulate up and down the spinal column between the crown and abdomen. The process is similar to kundalini energy. After many circulations *chi* is purified and then it transforms consciousness into mystical love. Male and female opposites are joined into a whole (physically and spiritually). This is exactly what happens in Indian philosophy - the union of Shiva and Shakti - produces enlightenment and illumination through the awakening of kundalini. *Chi* is known as *prana* in Hinduism.

The Caduceus, a wand entwined by two snakes and topped by wings, has been an esoteric symbol of spiritual enlightenment and intuitive wisdom since ancient times. Its shape is derived from the T-shaped cross used in Egyptian initiations. Its origin can be traced to Greco-Roman mythology dating back to 2600 BC. The Caduceus has

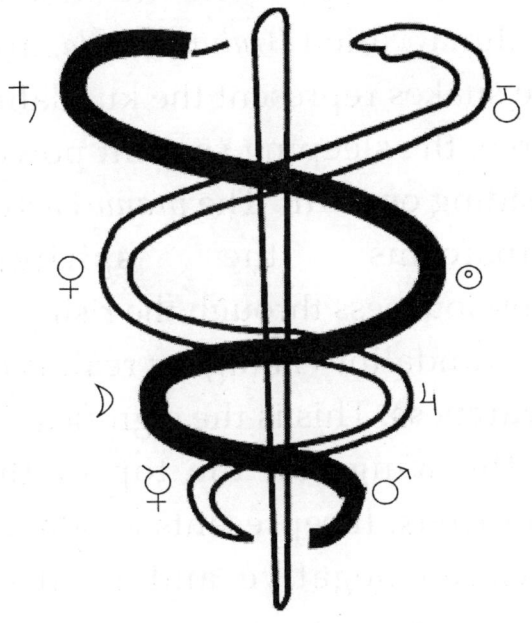

Caduceus

been a symbol of earth, water, fire and air in ancient Indian temples. The wand represents the stick of Brahma, called *Brahm Danda,* and the snakes represent the kundalini force, the sleeping serpent power residing on earth. The *pranic energy* transforms the spiritual consciousness through the rising of the kundalini via higher realms of awareness. This is the significance of the wings on the top of the Caduceus. It represents a balance between negative and positive forces in freemasonry.

Chakras, Nadis and Kundalini Yoga in other Faiths and Traditions

The phenomena of Chakras, Nadis and Kundalini is global. More or less in all religions you find the reference, of course, using different vocabulary. The oldest descriptions are found in Sanskrit and Tantric Buddhist teachings. "These teachings were old at the time of Jesus, and he brought some of them to early Christianity (Diane Stein, 1995, 77)."

And again, it has almost been lost in two thousand years and it is being reintroduced now. At some stage of time they were introduced to the healing art of Reiki in the East. As observed by Diane Stein, "Reiki is a Kundalini discipline (p. 84)." One becomes a Reiki healer by understanding the energy channels of the body and by learning to control the energy flows.

The Life Forces are called *prana* in India, *Ki* in Japan, *Chi* in China, and *Light* by channeller Barbara Marcianiak (1992). The methods of opening and channelling Ki are very ancient (Vajrayana Buddhism, Hinduism and Ch'i Kung), and it is believed that the Tantric God, Shiva, brought Reiki to the planet earth. Reiki is the vehicle of prana/ki/chi for transforming the individual, just as kundalini is. Getting Reiki is returning twelve-stranded DNA back to humans. Many Eastern teachings are being introduced to the West now.

Reiki/Kundalini reopens human abilities that have been forgotten for a long time. Reiki, however, takes only an attunement while other disciplines may take years of study and practise.

Just as Kundalini Shakti, called Mother Goddess brings consciousness into form; even so, Ki in Reiki is the Goddess of consciousness which sets a connection between the physical and spiritual through energy.

Kundalini is the female principle of existence even so, Chi on earth is the female principle representing Yin. Prana/Ki/Chi comes from the Heavens and is channelled into humans through meditation. The energy travels from the hand of the healer into the body of the person being healed.

Parallel to the concept of Kundalini being the creative force both in Heavens and on Earth, people are born with Heavenly Ki and, inward Ki is stored in human body between swadhishthan (pelvic chakra) and manipur (navel chakra), in the form portion of the body. This storage space in called 'Sacral Centre' in India, 'Triple warmer' in China and 'Hara' in Japan. All the three countries talk about the energy channels in the body through which Prana/Ki/Chi circulates.

In each system there is a central channel which is flanked by two other channels through which energy moves in opposite directions. The central line goes through the spinal column vertically, which is the path-way of the central power channel called Sushumna in India. There are seven energy stations on the central channel called "chakras." The chakra system exists on each of the etheric, emotional, mental and spiritual bodies. The three basic channels of energy branches that run throughout the body, like electrical wiring, provides energy to all parts of the body.

All the energy channels, main or branches, are called Nadis in India. From Nadis there is further division into physical central nervous system which is the autonomic system of the body.

The kundalini is supposed to be located on the etheric body. The central channel Sushumna, runs between the crown centre and root centre, and connects the energies of the universe and earth, and it contains a neutral charge in itself.

The other two channels are called Ida and Pingla, intertwining along Sushumna, the crossing points are

The Kundalini Channels and the Chakras

"Ida and Pingla, as they rise from the region of the coccyx, entwine around the Sushumna, crossing from side to side at nodes between the chakras... The small spiral pattern is seen in the double-helix configuration of the DNA molecule..."

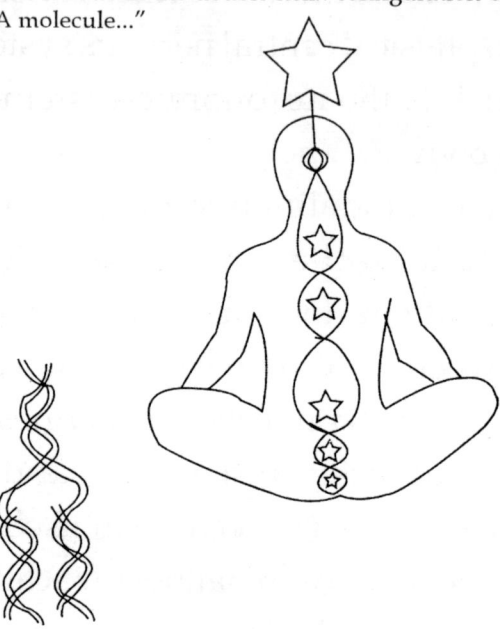

The double-helix configuration of the DNA molecule containing the generic code of life.

chakras or vortices of energy. Ida has downward movement on the front of the body and it is said to be feminine. Pingla rises upwards along the spinal column and is said to be masculine. Ida is supposed to have a cooling effect and it is compared with moon. Pingla is supposed to have heating effect and it is compared with sun.

In China, the two energy channels are considered to be the main trunk of acupuncture meridians. Just like the Nadis in India, the large and small energy channels are called the "acupuncture lines". The etheric body is connected to the physical body through these nerve channels which carry the Prana/Ki/Chi, thus forming a bridge.

Similarly, there is a bridge between the higher vibrational bodies and the etheric body through these channels. The nervous system channels or the meridians end up in reflexology points of the hands and feet, called 'seketsu' in Japan.

The three main channels are called by different names in China, Japan and other Asian countries but they serve the same purpose as the

Nadis in India. The most important Sushumna Nadi, which is the central channel and which goes beyond the physical and etheric levels, is called 'Hara Line' in Japan.

The other two channels are called 'conception or functional vessel' — and the 'governing or governor vessel', which are the Ida and Pingla in India. Parallel to the Indian concept, the Conception Vessel carries a negative energy charge and is feminine (Yin). Hui Yin point at the perineum is its starting point, moving upwards in front of the body/ and ending just below the lower lip. The Governing Vessel carries the positive charge and it is supposed to be masculine (Yang). A point between the genitals and anus is its beginning point, moving upwards along the spinal column at the back of the body, and ending at the top of the upper lip. (See figures on pages 107-111).

The emphasis is not placed on the etheric body where the chakras are located in Indian system, instead it is on the Hara Line. Thus, parallel to the chakras on the central channel, the acupuncture points hold key positions along the two energy channels in Asian systems.

These acupuncture points correspond to the positions of the chakras where the two Vessels (Ida and Pingla) cross each other. These points are the new chakras which together with the central channel are called the Hara Line.

In both the systems, the Prana/Ki moves spirally and is similar to the DNA life molecules. The awakening of kundalini in India is parallel to the movement of Prana/Ki through the energy channels in Asia, and is called Qi Gong or Chi Kung.

In India and Tibet the goal is transcendence of body and mind, and spiritual perfection; while in Asia it is replenishing the life force.

In Kundalini process, the Prana moves upwards from root centre to crown center. After the meeting of Shiva and Shakti at the Sahasrar, the energy is released and it returns through the same pathway by which it comes up. In Ki's movement, the downward path has equal importance. As a result the negative symptoms by the release of excessive energy are less as compared to the awakening of kundalini. In Kundalini process, the chakras are traversed along the Sushumna and its arrival at crown centre results in bliss, pure consciousness and transcendence of body and mind. It is the fusion of earth with heaven. Tantriks call it the union with Goddess.

In Asian system the discipline is milder in the sense that Ki moves in a circular path rather than up and down, and the results are aimed only at good health and long life, not at spiritual perfection. One aims to achieve freedom from diseases. The circular/movement of Ki is grounded every-time as compared to the rushing of Prana in upper centres. This avoids excessive accumulation of energy in the brain causing heating and other emotional problems.

In Asian process there is a feeling of safety valves in use, which is missing while energy returns in the Kundalini process. By moving energy through two channels in opposite direction, any excess energy is safely released (Chia, 1983, 6-7).

However, Kundalini is comparable to fast air travel carrying good results with some risks, while Reiki is safe and slow like land travel and with limited results.

Energy Flow through the Hara Line

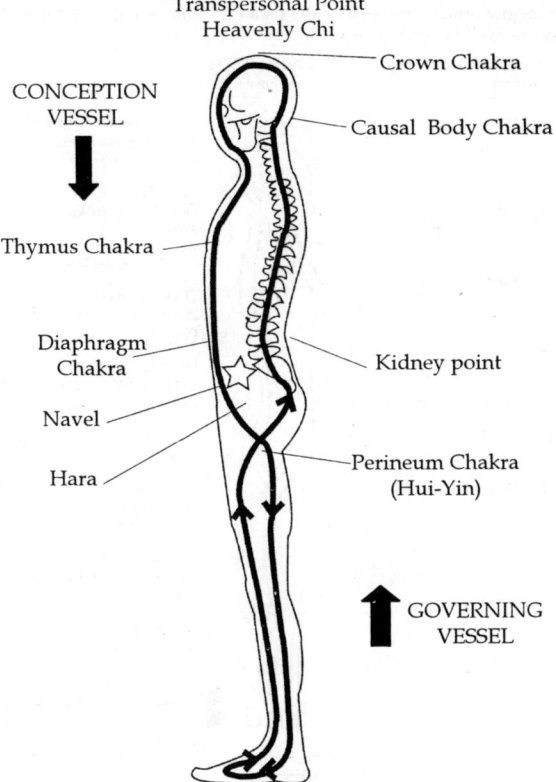

Circuit of Ki in the Body,[6] (continued)
The Microcosmic Orbit (The Great Heavenly Cycle)

The tongue touches the roof of the palate to complete the circuit of the Governor and Functional channels.

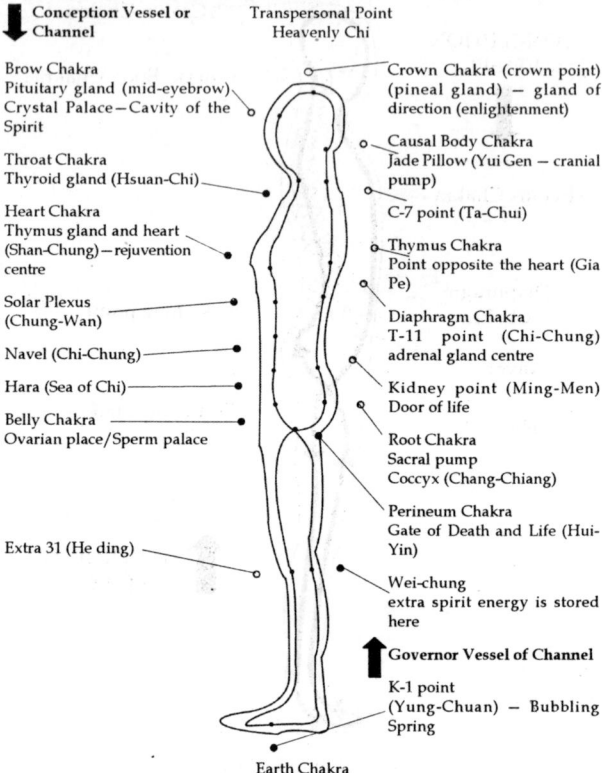

↓ Conception Vessel or Channel

Transpersonal Point
Heavenly Chi

Brow Chakra
Pituitary gland (mid-eyebrow)
Crystal Palace—Cavity of the Spirit

Throat Chakra
Thyroid gland (Hsuan-Chi)

Heart Chakra
Thymus gland and heart (Shan-Chung)—rejuvention centre

Solar Plexus
(Chung-Wan)

Navel (Chi-Chung)

Hara (Sea of Chi)

Belly Chakra
Ovarian place/Sperm palace

Extra 31 (He ding)

Crown Chakra (crown point) (pineal gland) – gland of direction (enlightenment)

Causal Body Chakra
Jade Pillow (Yui Gen – cranial pump)

C-7 point (Ta-Chui)

Thymus Chakra
Point opposite the heart (Gia Pe)

Diaphragm Chakra
T-11 point (Chi-Chung) adrenal gland centre

Kidney point (Ming-Men)
Door of life

Root Chakra
Sacral pump
Coccyx (Chang-Chiang)

Perineum Chakra
Gate of Death and Life (Hui-Yin)

Wei-chung
extra spirit energy is stored here

↑ Governor Vessel of Channel

K-1 point
(Yung-Chuan) – Bubbling Spring

Earth Chakra

Circuit of Ki in the Body
The Microcosmic Orbit
Small Heavenly Cycle
Front View of the Small Heavenly Cycle

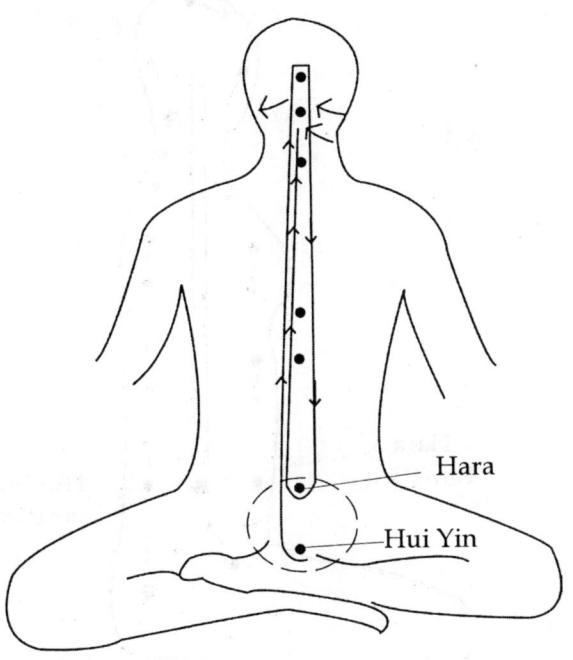

Circuit of Ki in the Body
The Microcosmic Orbit
Small Heavenly Cycle
Side View of the Small Heavenly Cycle

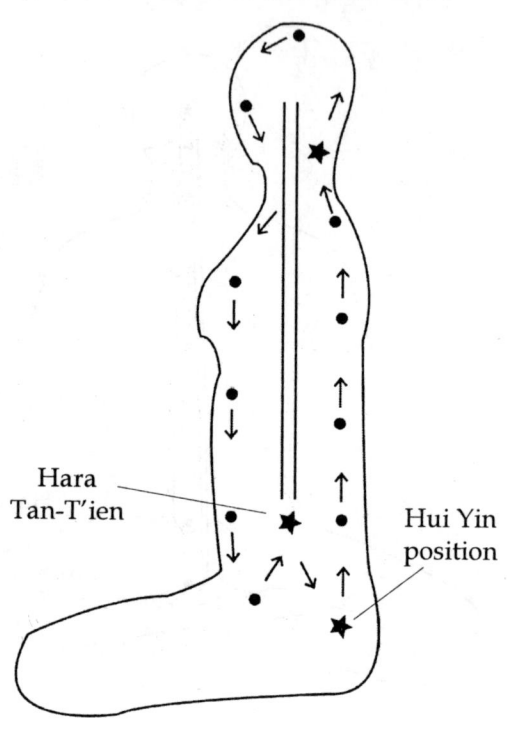

The Hara Line

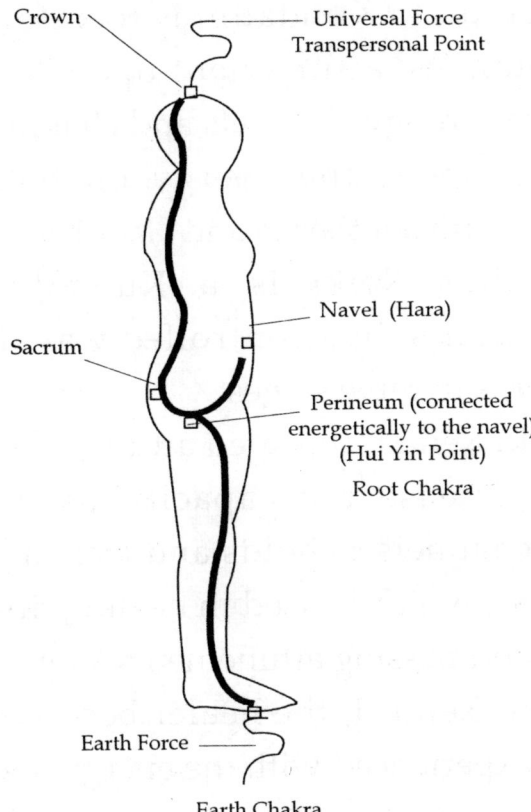

An alternative and milder method to Kundalini is therefore Reiki. Its attunement opens the three energy channels and chakras, and opens the energy on both Sushumna (etheric) and Hara levels.

Thus Reiki is a Kundalini discipline in a controlled way. It works in three stages:

- In Reiki I, repeated attunements increase the capacity of the channels to holds and transmit Ki, which is used in healing first and passing attunements later.
- In Reiki II, the healer becomes experienced with the energy and begins to manipulate it. While

healing, a strong amount of Ki passes through the healer at this stage.

- In Reiki III, the healer has to learn to transmit energy at will and at the same time be conscious of what is happening. Slowly, mind and intention are added to the process.

In all Tantric practices in India, Tibet, and Japan, Reiki has been a part of the long training. In China the awareness of the pattern of flow of energy is called 'The Microcosmic Orbit' in the discipline of Ch'i Kung. There are exercises for the generation and use of energy, and many of them are common in Ch'i Kung and Kundalini Yoga. For details in Ch'i Kung one can refer to the books:

- *Awaken Healing Energy Through the Tao*, Mantak Chia, Aurora Press, 1983.
- *Awaken Healing Light of the Tao*, Mantak and Mannewan Chia, Healing Tao Books, 1993.
- *Essential Reiki – A Complete Guide to an Ancient Healing Art*, Diane Stein, The Crossing Press Inc..., 1995.

Preparatory Microcosmic Orbit

It is required to increase the ability of the body, also as to receive and channel Ki. It is a preparation for the proper exercise to be discussed next. It connects the Conception and Governing vessels and a complete energy circle is set up in the body. It is done by focusing the energy inwardly or in meditation.

- Bring your awareness to the Hara or the navel. After a while warmth will be felt which indicates the building of Ki.

- Move your awareness to the root chakra or Hui Yin and then up towards the spinal column. Stop for a while at the Ming-Men point (kidney level) and then guide the Ki upwards to the crown centre (pineal gland).
- There should be no forcing but a smooth flowing of the energy. Hold the energy at the crown centre for about ten minutes and then bring the awareness to Ajna chakra (third Eye - pituitary gland).
- Continue the downward flow of energy to navel region or Hara. Hold it for a while till warmth is

felt, and then restart the orbit by moving to the root chakra.

- Repeat the cycle as many times as conveniently possible and slowly increase to 36 rounds at each sitting.

This should be continued till you achieve some proficiency. Then include the exercise to set up connection legs and earth. Move energy with awareness from navel to root centre (Hui Yin).

- Now divide the energy into two parts and send one down to the back of the thigh, to the back of the knees.

- Next direct it to the calves of the legs, to the soles of the feet.
- The chakras are located on the soles at Yung Chuan (K-1 acupuncture point) called, 'Bubbling Spring' which connects the body electrically to earth's energy.
- When the soles get warm enough, move Ki to the big toes, then to the knees through the front of the feet. Remember that the energy is to be drawn from the earth through the soles. The flow up, inside the things and back, should be continued, to the Hui Yin or Root centre.

- Now the Ki should be sent back up the spinal column and, at a point between the shoulder blades it should be divided for the arms. Let it off to the inside of the two arms, to the middle of the palms.
- Be aware of the sensation and take the flow along the middle finger to the upper side of the arms outwardly.
- Reaching the shoulders it goes back to the main circuit and to the crown through the spine and neck.
- Return to Hara through central channel. 'Grounding is the

concluding part of the exercise, which collects the energy and prevents electrical overload and discomfort (Chia, 1986, 59)'. Hara is the starting and stopping place of energy.

- Place your fist lightly over navel region and rub it in a spiral position for upto 6 inches width.
- For women the spiral should be moved 36 times counter clockwise, then 24 times clockwise. For men it is reverse, that is, 36 times clockwise and then 24 times counterclockwise.

We shall now be describing the two important exercises that are common to Kundalini Yoga and Ch'i Kung. They appear to have come from India and Tibet to China and Asia. These exercises have health-increasing value on one hand and spiritual value on the other.

Hindu and Buddhists believe that the karma can be resolved only when you are in human form, and this is the importance of human birth. One can see that things like Reiki too can only be done when you have a physical body. I have stated elsewhere that the psychic being, which links soul to super-soul is also available in human form.

Certain things that dampen the effect of Reiki, and other spiritual practices for that matter, are smoking, drugs and alcohol. One should not do Reiki when one is under the influence of these things, it negates the sacredness of the channel.

First Exercise

Begin with the Microcosmic Orbit while in the meditative state. Become aware of Ki as fire energy (Raku) and move it from navel (Hara) to root (Hui Yin) and then up the spinal column to the crown centre. Let the energy come down to Hara through the front of the body.

For Women
- Sit in Siddha-Yoni-asana, that is, sitting on the floor, the heel of one foot should be pressing the Root chakra (against vagina) and

the heel of the other foot presenting the Swadhishthan chakra (above clitoris).
- Now apply moolbandha (root lock). Next place your tongue against the roof of the mouth behind the teeth (khechari mudra). Sometimes sitting on a small pillow can help to observe this asana. Now rub the two hands against each other to get warmth.
- Massage your bare breasts with your warmed palms in an upward and outward direction. Take care that the nipples are not

stimulated and repeat the practice 18 times.
- Feel the flow of Ki in the Root chakra (vagina), Crown chakra (pineal gland) and Ajna chakra (Third Eye).
- Upwards rotation is called dispersion. Make the energy flow from breasts, vagina, crown centre and ajna chakras to anahata chakra (Heart centre) by stopping with the fingers lightly touching the nipples, while performing dispersion.
- The set of 18 massage circles should be repeated 2 to 4 times.

Each time, make Ki flow to the heart centre.
- The direction of rotations should now be reversed, that is moving down and inward instead of up and out. This is inversion. The energy should be gathered into the nipples and moved to spine at the back of the breasts.
- The set of 18 circles should be repeated 2 to 4 times.
- Now move the hands from breasts to kidney point at the back of the body, behind the lower ribs.
- The area should now be massaged and lightly shaken

Ki Exercise for Women
Exercise One (Continued)

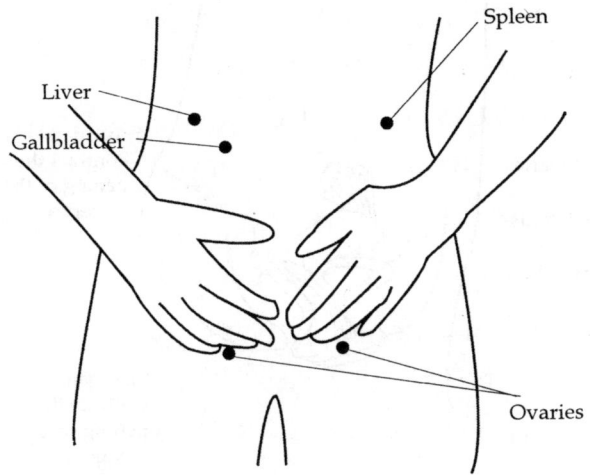

Massage the groin and waist

Ki Exercise for Women
Exercise One (Continued)

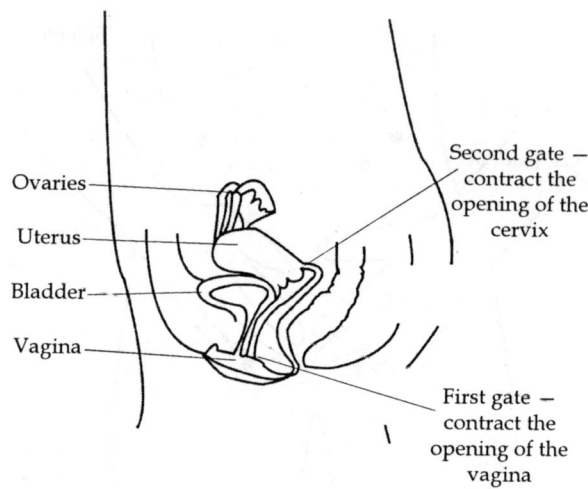

The Hui Yin position — Gate of Life and Death for Women

Ki Exercise for Women
Exercise One

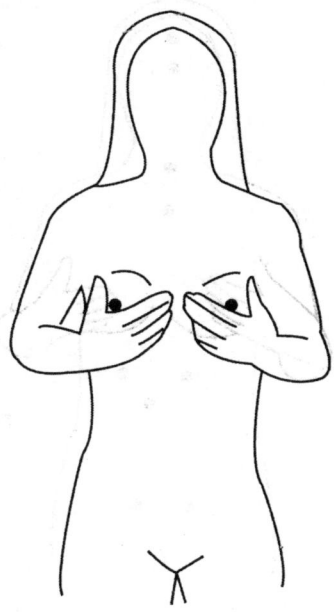

Massage breasts in an upward and outward direction

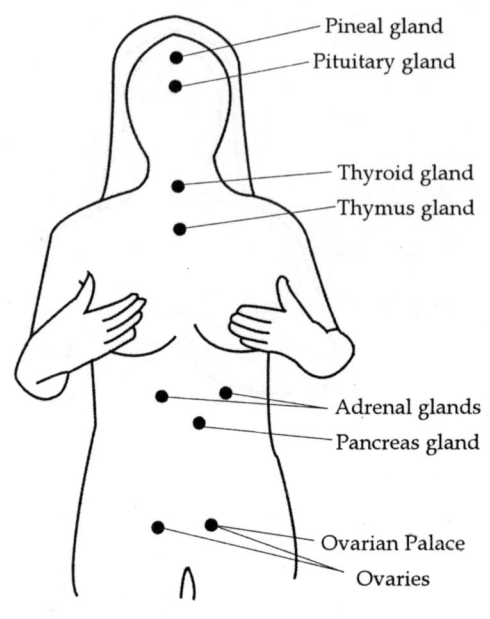

Touch the nipples and bring the energy into the heart

upto 18 times, and with a little rest, the process should be repeated 2 to 4 times. Be aware of the warmth in the kidney region.
- Next massage the lower abdomen from the groin to the ovaries, the liver and gall bladder on the right side under the lower ribs, and then the spleen on the left side.
- The outward and inward massage should be performed 36 times in each set.
- Then the vagina should be massaged to store the energy. With little pause, be aware of the expansion of Ki.

- Now place your right hand on your vagina and left hand on anahat chakras (heart center), be aware of the universal love being created, and draw it into the heart.
- Pull the Earth energy in, continue the Microcosmic Orbit, and end with the storage of energy into the Hara.
- This is the end of the first exercise for women.

Remarks

It is not only opening of the Nadis and activation of Kundalini, but the conversion of sexual energy into spiritual force and universal love, that is the result of these exercises. Sexual energy is lost in menstruation, ovulation and copulation. Reiki exercise recycles the energy and converts it into Ki to produce peace, inner happiness, physical well-being and freedom from disease. It also balances hormonal processes in women. Menopause symptoms may disappear with dispersion rotations. It results in "turning back of the blood." The lumps may disappear too.

Dispersion rotation tends to decrease the breast size, while inversion rotations increase breast size. If both rotations are performed same number of times, hormones are balanced without altering the breast size. The most important happening is the redirection of sexual Ki towards crown centre. It is associated with the stopping of the menstruation cycle. However, if you want to get pregnant, reduce the number of rotations, say below 100 everyday. There is no side effect, ageing is arrested, and creativity and mental awareness are increased.

Caution

Applying moolbandha (Root lock) while sitting in Siddha-Yoni-asana may produce heat and even bring orgasm from the pressure above and below the clitoris.

Note

Reversal of the flow of sexual energy from moving "down and out" to moving "in and up" enriches the brain and makes it strong enough to receive "enlightenment". A man or woman in whom this has happened, is called "urdhvareta" in Sanskrit, and is said to be a successful yogi who has achieved "liberation".

For Men

- Perform Microcosmic Orbit in meditative state with bare body, gathering Ki energy in the hara region.
- Rub your hands against each other, and when they become warm, massage and lightly shake the kidneys upto 18 times. Pause and feel the heat.
- Feel that you are inhaling through the kidneys and exhaling Ki into the Kidney Point.

- The process should be repeated 2 to 4 times. Bring awareness to the energy connection between the kidneys and the genitals.
- Bring heat to your hands again by rubbing.
- Hold the testicles lightly by cupping them in one palm without squeezing, and cover them with the other palm. The testicles should now be massaged upto 36 times and then the gathering of Ki in the testicles should be felt.
- Holding the testicles in the left palm, place your right over Hara.

- Massage the navel with your hand, clockwise 36 to 81 times.
- Produce heat by rubbing the hands, then change the position by cupping with right palm and massaging the Hara with left hand, counterclockwise 36 to 81 times.
- Cover the genitals with two palms, feel the stimulation in the organs, and gather Ki by contracting the muscles.
- Pause and be aware of the expansion of the energy.
- Keep right hand over the testicles and left on the Anahat chakra. (Heart centre).

Ki Exercise for men

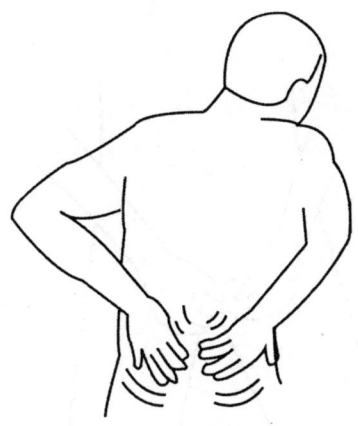

Massage and tap the kidneys.

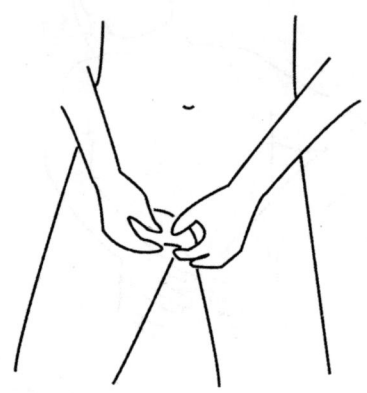

Massage the testicles

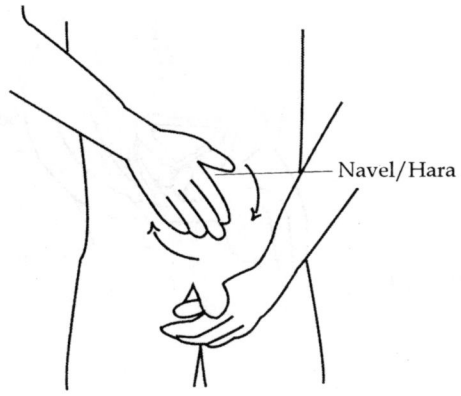

The left hand holds the testicles. The right hand massages the abdomen clockwise.

Location of Hui Yin Position for men.

- Feel the presence of universal love and draw the energy into your heart.
- Return the energy to Hara by the continuation of Microcosmic Orbit, and end the exercise with grounding.

All details can be remembered from the exercise for woman. Benefits are all the same as for woman. Additionally, men get relieved from premature ejaculation, prostate problems and other sexual difficulties, and the sexual organs become stronger. Reversal of sexual energy makes one "Hurdhvareta" and provides liberation ultimately. One achieves inner peace, increased creativity and mental awareness, spiritual growth and freedom from disease.

Second Exercise

The *Hui Yin Position* connects the Conception and Governing Vessels at the top and bottom of the body. This is done in two steps.

Step I
Sit in Siddhasana (men) or Siddha-yoni-asana (women) and locate the point in between anus and genitals. This is mooladhara chakra, (India) or acupuncture point called CV-I (Conception Vessel-I). In Kung, it is called the gate of Life and Death.

Step II

Apply Khechari Mudra by placing the tongue on the roof of the mouth, just behind the teeth. This connects the Conception and Governing Vessels at the top of the body, just as the perineum contraction does at the root. Just touch the palate with the tongue tip and keep it in place during the exercise.

For Women
- Apply moolbandh by contracting the muscles of the vagina and anus. If you contract anus as if drawing the rectum up into the body, the vaginal muscles will follow automatically.

- Then contract the vaginal muscles as if trying to stop the flow of urine.
- One also does so to stimulate the orgasm, so it should be known. You may feel as if air is entering through rectum.
- Hold the position as long as convenient and then release. Repeat the process a couple of times. It may be difficult in the beginning, but with practice you will be able to hold it conveniently for longer periods of time.

- The Hui Yin Position is held, simultaneously touching the roof of the mouth with tip of the tongue, and holding the breath too for two to three minutes, as long as you are passing the Reiki attunements.
- Muscular control is the goal of the exercise. Ki begins to flow upwards along the Hara Line, and it cannot flow downwards. A connection is made to the Earth energy by drawing it upwards into the Hara.
- Holding Hui Yin position, and tongue at the roof of the mouth,

the circuit is closed and the Conception and Governing Vessels are joined at both ends. Microcosmic Orbit begins to operate almost immediately.

- Ki begins to move downward from the Crown, and upward from the earth. Hara is activated and energy circulates in the body as if making the figure of 8.
- Keep the three parts of Hui Yin at hold: Contracting vaginal and anus muscles, placing the tongue on the roof of the mouth, and holding a deep breath, Microcosmic Orbit becomes possible now.

For Men
- Sitting is Siddhasana apply moolbandh by contracting the muscles of anus, put the tip of the tongue at the roof of the mouth, and hold a deep breath, as long conveniently possible. Rest of the things for men and women are the same.
- Both men and women should practise the exercise morning and evening. As the period increases, the state of total well being sets in and becomes a part of daily life.

All other advantages stated earlier begin to come. First exercise is for removing energy blockages, increasing spiritual awareness and developing the body-mind-spirit connection. Second exercise is for passing Reiki attunements.

This is the end of Kundalini Yoga. However, with the practise of the Microcosmic Orbit and two Ki exercises, you are ready for Reiki III.

OTHER TITLES IN THE SERIES

All You Wanted to Know About

Gems
Graphology
Numerology
Palmistry
Astrology
Vaastushastra
Feng Shui
Hypnosis
Dowsing
Increasing Memory Power
The Prophecies of Nostradamus